I'm a little scientist!

I CAN CHANGE THE WORLD...

See a QR code? Scan it to access bonus resources!

WITH THE TOSS OF A BOTTLE

BY
RONALD CHAN

ILLUSTRATED BY
YEEWEARN

WS Education

NEW JERSEY · LONDON · SINGAPORE · BEIJING · SHANGHAI · HONG KONG · TAIPEI · CHENNAI · TOKYO

One afternoon, Ms Prakash and Mr Sohn were out with their class on a field trip. As they strolled along an idyllic boardwalk, Ms Prakash explained the important role of mangroves.

Class, look at these mangroves! Did you know that they protect our coasts from tides and waves? They're also home to many fascinating creatures like horseshoe crabs and snakes!

The class continued along the boardwalk as Ms Prakash discussed how global warming can affect coastal environments. Just then, Mr Sohn spotted something happening in the distance.

Now, children, we must protect our shores. Climate change can cause our sea levels to rise dramatically, and we have to...

"My friends," Mr Sohn said, "your bottles don't belong in the sea. This recycling bin for used plastics is where they should go!" He gestured behind the teenagers to a row of recycling bins. One of the teens shook her head, a disbelieving look on her face.

"It's not all just fun and games," Mr Sohn said sternly. "We have to be responsible citizens of Earth too!"

"That's right," Ms Prakash chimed in, as she and the class joined them. "Did you know that with the toss of a bottle, you can change the world?" The teens looked at the bottle, puzzled.

You must be kidding. How can we change the world with this?

"Get on the Soaring Sampan! Let's find out what a stray bottle could do to our world," Ms Prakash said, as she ushered the class and the teenagers into the mobile classroom.

As the Soaring Sampan descended into the surrounding water, Ms Prakash pointed to some struggling creatures and exclaimed, "Look at those animals! Our plastic trash has trapped them and they're unable to move."

Oh dear, that bird might really end up eating a plastic spoon.

Mr Sohn gazed into the turquoise water and continued, "By discarding our bottles and other plastic waste in the right place, we can keep them out of our rivers and oceans, and protect our wildlife!"

Wow, see how happy those animals are to be free!

MEET BAILEY,

a cormorant who plies the coasts. Seabirds like cormorants are often victims of debris like plastic utensils and even balloons! They either mistake the debris for food or get trapped in it while they hunt for actual food. Help Bailey out by tossing your used bottles in the right bin!

! By disposing of our trash properly, we prevent them from leaking into these ecosystems, and we can also keep our water bodies clean!

Hundreds of fish species have been observed to ingest some form of plastic.

"Plastic products break down very gradually over up to hundreds of years," Ms Prakash explained, as the Soaring Sampan turned inland. "However, when they do, they form microplastics, or very small bits of plastic. Some are smaller than the width of a strand of hair!"

Although plastics take a long time to break down, they eventually do. They fragment into smaller pieces called microplastics. Microplastics can be very difficult to detect and are still not well understood.

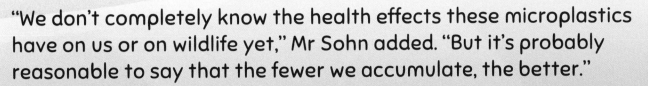

"We don't completely know the health effects these microplastics have on us or on wildlife yet," Mr Sohn added. "But it's probably reasonable to say that the fewer we accumulate, the better."

MEET FAIZAL,

a barramundi being bred in an open–sea farm. Fish like Faizal can mistake microplastics for food. These plastic specks are short on calories and could cause fish to lose their appetite or be more vulnerable to predators. Less plastic trash in oceans means fewer microplastics eaten by Faizal!

! However, while fish can consume microplastics and seawater may contain them, they mostly do not enter the fish tissues we might eat and are generally filtered out by water treatment plants.

Ms Prakash steered the Soaring Sampan over a section of the city with various garbage disposal facilities.

So, Mr Sohn, if we don't want these plastic products to end up in rivers and oceans, or anywhere else they shouldn't be... should we discard them in a rubbish bin instead?

! There are no ideal ways to dispose of plastics. They can sit in landfills for a very long time.

Plastic Bag: **20** YEARS

Plastic Bottle: **450** YEARS

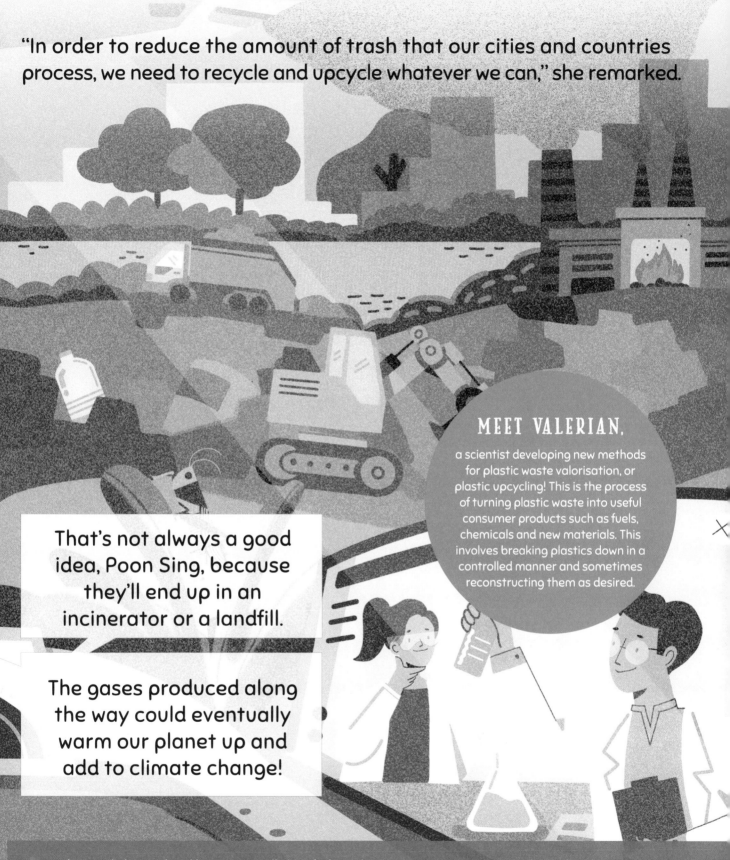

"In order to reduce the amount of trash that our cities and countries process, we need to recycle and upcycle whatever we can," she remarked.

That's not always a good idea, Poon Sing, because they'll end up in an incinerator or a landfill.

The gases produced along the way could eventually warm our planet up and add to climate change!

MEET VALERIAN,

a scientist developing new methods for plastic waste valorisation, or plastic upcycling! This is the process of turning plastic waste into useful consumer products such as fuels, chemicals and new materials. This involves breaking plastics down in a controlled manner and sometimes reconstructing them as desired.

! When sunlight, wind and heat eventually break them down, some may generate methane that warms our planet, while others may form microplastics that can get transported to other places. Incinerators can burn plastics up, but the gases and ashes produced can be toxic and must be treated carefully.

"That means we have to discard our used bottles in a recycling bin, right?" a student asked, as the Soaring Sampan glided over a shopping mall.

MALL

Thank you for bringing your own reusable bag!

Oh dear, I've taken a lot of single-use plastic bags today. I'll try to recycle them later or reuse them to hold trash at home!

I'll bring mine the next time too!

! Remember the phrase, "Reduce, Reuse, Recycle"? The order is important! Once our plastic items are worn out, let's try to recycle them if possible, instead of simply throwing them into the trash.

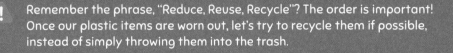

REDUCE   REUSE   RECYCLE

"Exactly, Sarah," Mr Sohn nodded. "We want to recycle these used plastics as much as possible! But plastics are sometimes difficult to recycle. Perhaps we can find better ways to use them."

Hmm, which bin does this bottle go into?

However, recycling can sometimes be a technically and logistically challenging process, so we should focus on reducing and reusing whenever we can. Can you think of ways for us to reduce and reuse plastics?

There are many different types of plastics, each with its own recycling method.

1 PETE   4 LDPE   5 PP

"Yes, Mr Sohn! If plastics can last for decades and centuries, why limit them to minutes of usage?" Ms Prakash chipped in as a food centre came into view.

So, remember, "Reduce, Reuse, Recycle"! If we can reduce our usage of plastics, that would be the best. However, if we have to use them, why not try to reuse them as much as possible?

Finally, Ms Prakash walked to the front of the Soaring Sampan and asked everyone, "So, class, what have you learnt today?"

IMPROPERLY DISCARDED

- Harm wildlife
- Generate microplastics

SENT TO LANDFILLS AND INCINERATORS

- Undesirable by-products

Plastics can harm wildlife and possibly also affect our lives if they're not disposed of properly!

SINGLE-USE PRODUCTS

NOT ALWAYS EASY
TO RECYCLE

· USE REUSABLE
PRODUCTS!

We need to discard our used plastics in the right place to keep our environment clean.

And better yet, let's use reusable products whenever we can!

Be Plastic Savers, like Us!

COMPLETE MS PRAKASH'S LESSON!

Ms Prakash was about to tell us what we could do to respond to sea level rise, when Mr Sohn caught the teenagers almost tossing bottles into the sea.

Can you complete Ms Prakash's sentence by thinking of what the consequences of sea level rise on shorelines are, and what we could do (or not do) to prevent them? Some hints are shown below!

Climate change can cause our sea levels to rise dramatically, and we have to _____ _____.

CONSEQUENCES:

Stronger storm surges and higher tides erode coasts.

MITIGATING ACTIONS:

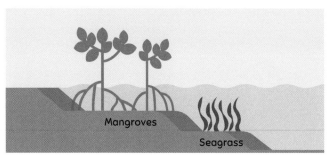

Grow mangroves and seagrass to keep the soil firm and withstand erosion (and absorb carbon dioxide).

Higher sea levels flood coastal homes.

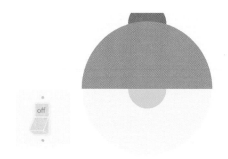

Switch off unused lights at home to reduce carbon dioxide generation.

DID YOU NOTICE?

 Did you notice these during the field trip? These can help us to build a more sustainable world!

 **Lights with solar panels (Pg5):** It's not easy to build facilities in nature reserves without being intrusive on the surroundings! Solar panels receive and convert energy directly from the Sun to light up the boardwalk. They also do not generate carbon dioxide and add to global warming.

Sort your waste (Pg7): Treating, recycling and upcycling waste becomes much easier when you sort it before you bin it. If you encounter waste and recycling bins with different categories, use the right bin for each type of trash!

Saving energy (Pg18): Did you know that treating water and incinerating rubbish consume a lot of electricity? By reducing the amount of trash we generate, we can treat our water more easily and burn less waste, and thus reduce the amount of electricity we use.

Some of our current electricity generation methods still produce carbon dioxide, so saving energy often means keeping our planet cool!

 Can you think of other ways to lead a more sustainable lifestyle and maintain a healthier planet?

LET'S REDUCE AND REUSE!

The table shows some common household items made with single-use plastics. Can you think of durable and reusable versions of these plastic products? Fill in your answers in the right column.

⭐ **Hint:** They need not be made of plastic! Some of these have appeared in the story too.

SINGLE-USE PLASTIC PRODUCT	REUSABLE VERSION?
Bag	
Fork	
Bottle	
Takeaway Food Container	
Coffee Cup	

Look again at your answers. How can you incorporate them into your daily life? Can you convince others to help you with your efforts?

HOW CAN I GET OTHERS TO JOIN IN?

Here's how you can encourage those around you to learn more about plastic pollution and wastage, and how to reduce them:

Help clean up your local waterways:
Ocean plastics begin as river, canal and beach plastics. Rope in your friends to volunteer for clean-up efforts at your local nature areas and beaches, and help to stem the seaward flow of plastic trash!

Reach out to your local stores:
Stores are a key distributor of single-use plastics such as vegetable wrappers, food packaging and shopping bags. Write in to your local stores or visit them, and encourage them to adopt more sustainable packaging and sell product refills for soap and stationery.

Create a zero-waste, "Bring Your Own" community:
Encourage your peers and family to start a zero-waste lifestyle! Make it a point to bring your own reusable bags and support local products with less packaging, say no to disposable utensils and bring your own containers when you order food and drinks together!

What other ways are there to help and to spread the word?

Published by

WS Education, an imprint of
World Scientific Publishing Co. Pte. Ltd.
5 Toh Tuck Link, Singapore 596224
USA office: 27 Warren Street, Suite 401–402, Hackensack, NJ 07601
UK office: 57 Shelton Street, Covent Garden, London WC2H 9HE

National Library Board, Singapore Cataloguing in Publication Data
Name(s): Chan, Ronald, author. | Yee Wearn, illustrator.
Title: I can change the world ... with the toss of a bottle / written by Ronald Chan ; illustrated by Yeewearn.
Other Title(s): I'm a scientist! (WS Education (Firm))
Description: Singapore : WS Education, [2022]
Identifier(s): ISBN 978-981-12-5755-1 (hardback) | 978-981-12-5756-8 (paperback) |
    978-981-12-5757-5 (ebook for institutions) | 978-981-12-5758-2 (ebook for individuals)
Subject(s): LCSH: Recycling (Waste, etc.)--Juvenile fiction. | Sustainable living--Juvenile fiction.
Classification: DDC 428.6--dc23

British Library Cataloguing-in-Publication Data
A catalogue record for this book is available from the British Library.

For any available supplementary material, please visit
https://www.worldscientific.com/worldscibooks/10.1142/12881#t=suppl

Printed in Singapore